I WILL LOVE YOU LITTLE ONE

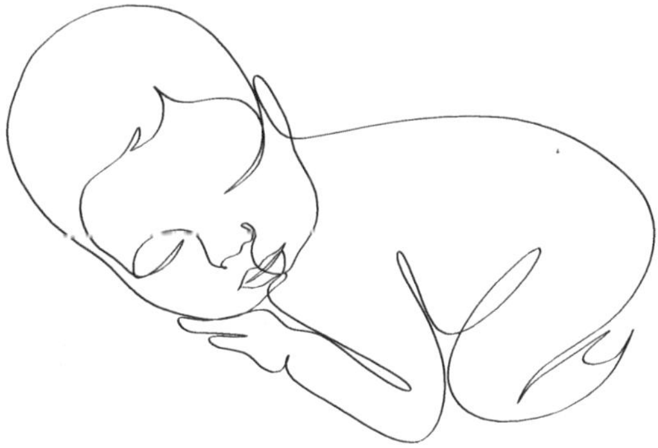

Olivia Calaway

I will love you little one

Like the rivers love the seas

Like the birds love the trees

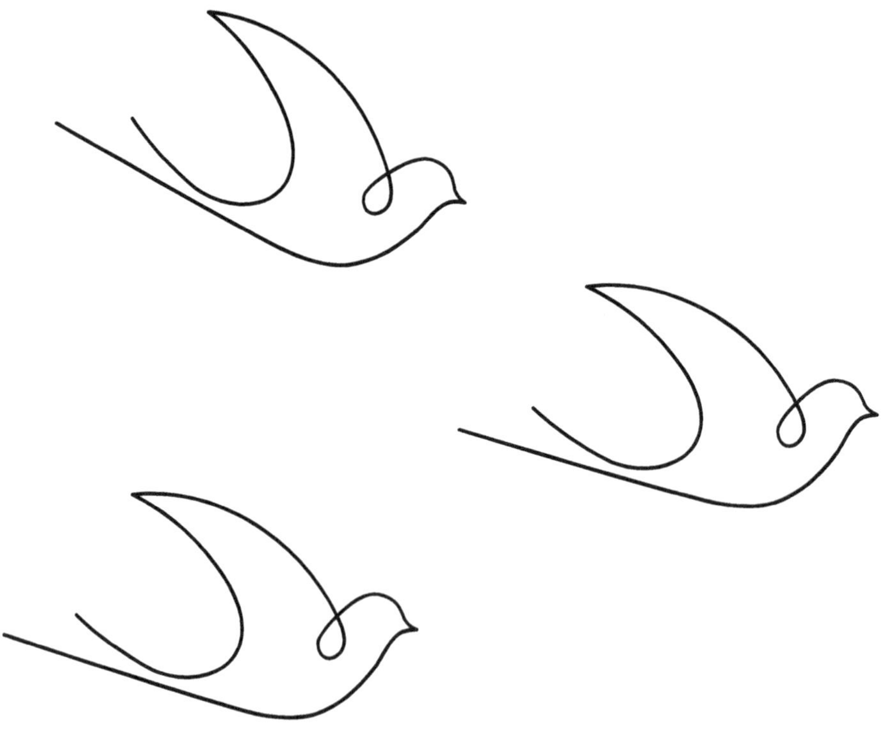

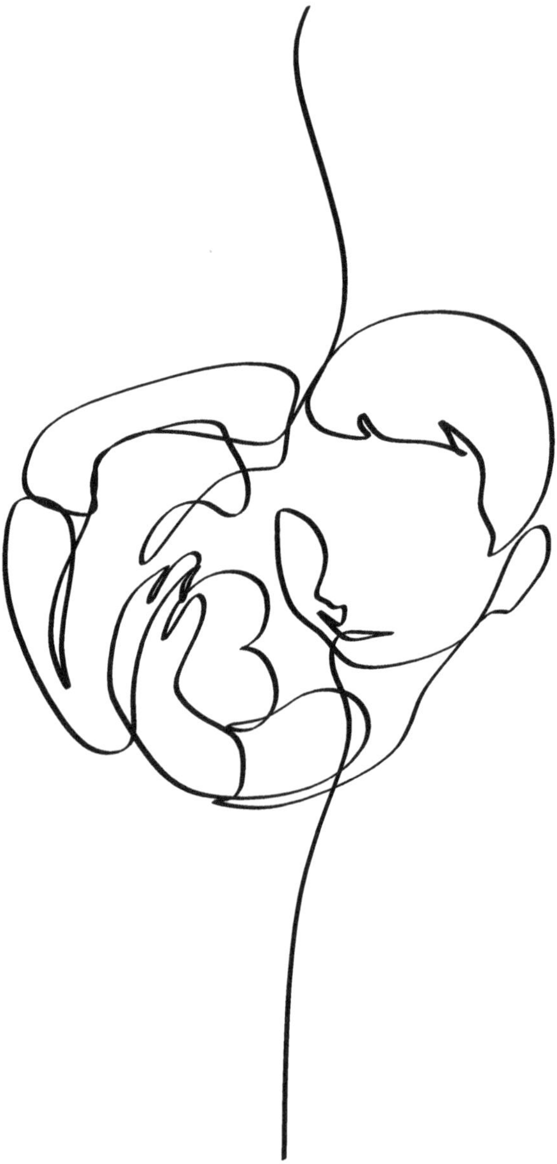

I will love you like the sun
hugs the clouds

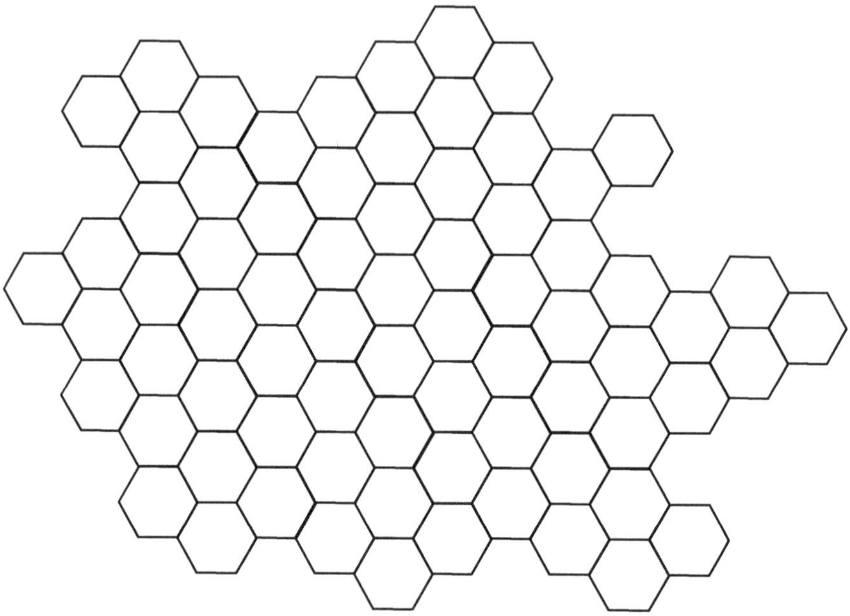

And I will tell the world like
the buzz of the bees

You little one are more
precious than these

I will care for you with
the tenderest touch

I will tell you, " you are more than enough"

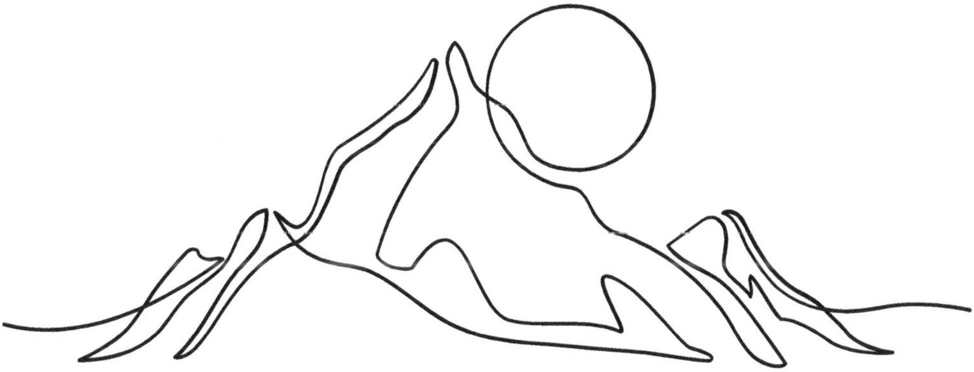

Just like the sun falls and the moon always shines—my love for you will never end as surely as the sun will rise

I will love you when both of
your hands fit in one of mine

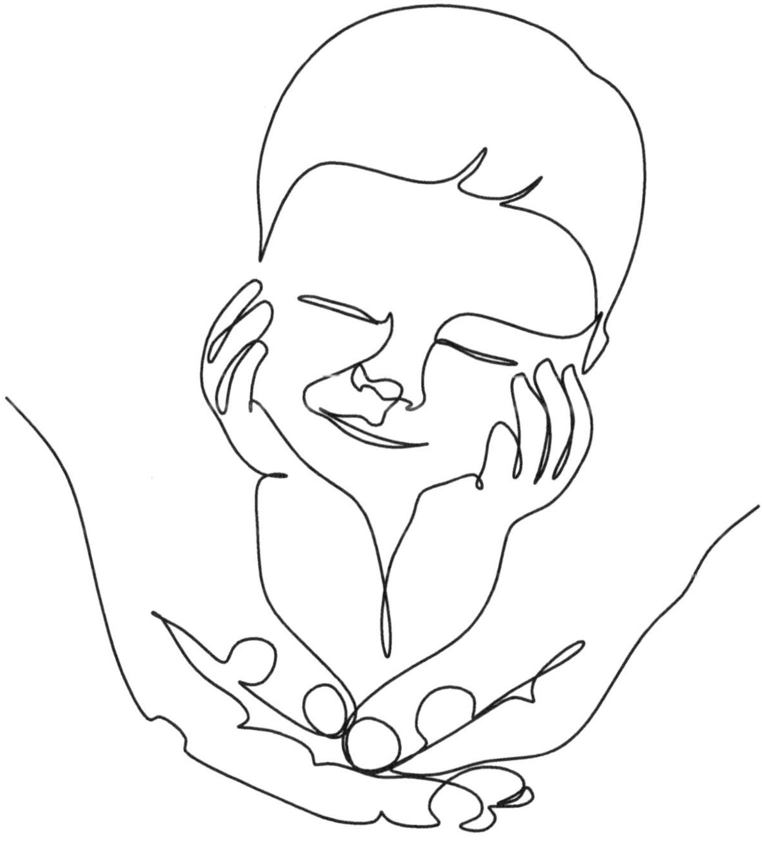

I will love you still when you
hold little hands of your own
I will look back to see how
much you have grown

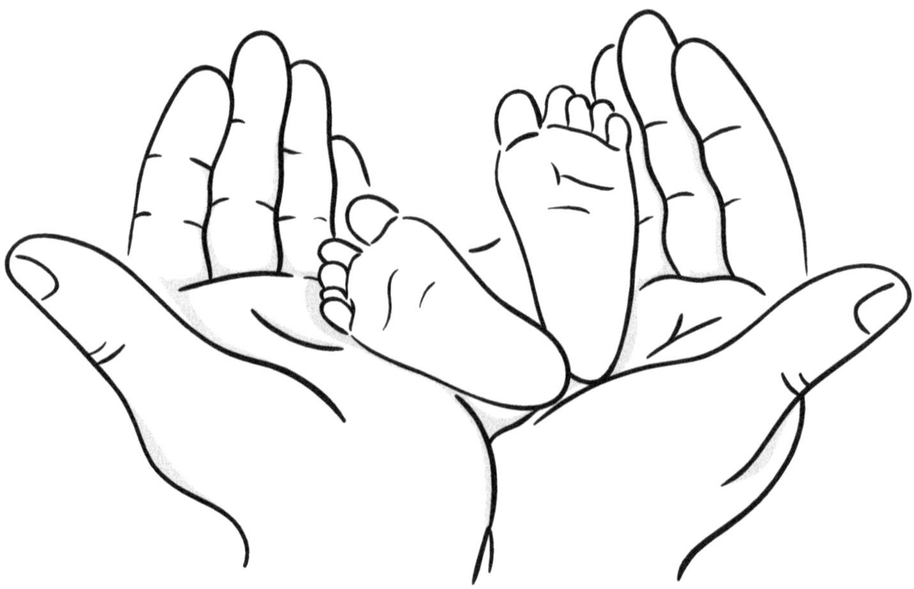

I love you little one from the first moment I knew...

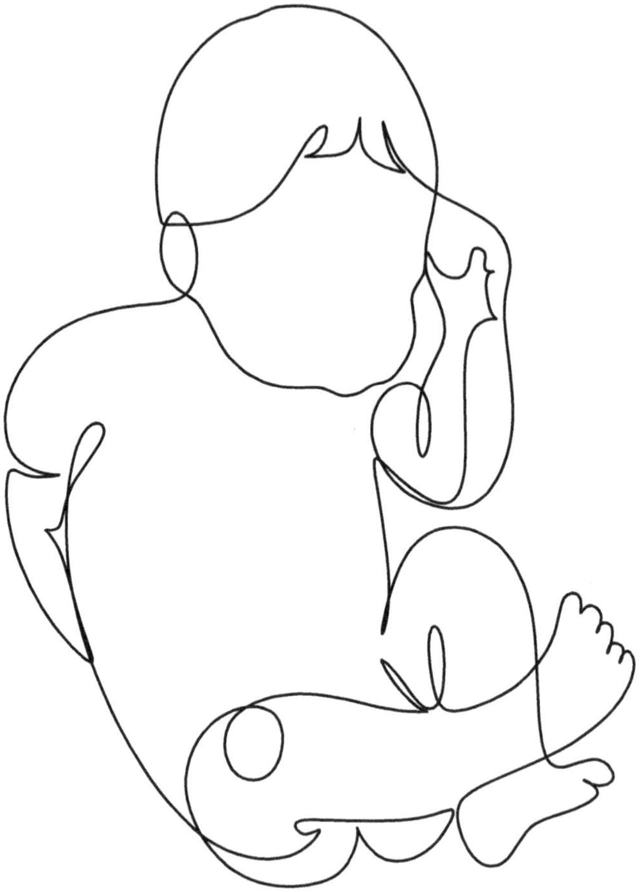

God gave me you because
He loves me too

" For you created my inmost being; you knit me together in my mother's womb. I praise you because I am fearfully and wonderfully made; your works are wonderful, I know that full well. My frame was not hidden from you when I was made in the secret place, when I was woven together in the depths of the earth. Your eyes saw my unformed body; all the days ordained for me were written in your book before one of them came to be. How precious to me are your thoughts, God! How vast is the sum of them!"

Psalms 139:13-17

www.ingramcontent.com/pod-product-compliance
Ingram Content Group UK Ltd.
Pitfield, Milton Keynes, MK11 3LW, UK
UKHW062155030826
14089UKWH00026B/40

9 798868 920165